The Just Girl Project

BOOK OF ASTROLOGY

A GUIDE FOR
EVERY RELATIONSHIP
& SITUATIONSHIP

ILANA HARKAVY AND BRIANNA RAUCHMAN

ILLUSTRATIONS BY ERICA LEWIS

SPRUCE BOOKS
A Sasquatch Books Imprint

DEDICATED TO OUR PARENTS,
WHO PROBABLY DON'T
UNDERSTAND ASTROLOGY BUT
WILL LOVE OUR BOOK ANYWAY. 🩶

CONTENTS

WELCOME TO ASTROLAND   *1*

DATING   **4**

SITUATIONSHIPS   **32**

RELATIONSHIPS   **52**

HEARTBREAK   **80**
AND HEALING

FRIENDSHIPS   **100**

FAMILY   **120**

ACKNOWLEDGMENTS   *138*

♎ LIBRA ♏ SCORPIO ♐ SAG ♑ CAP ♒ AQUARIUS ♓ PISCES

HEY, GIRL!

You know that super-annoying friend who you call when you just had a date that went terribly wrong? And you're all "OMG, they didn't blah blah blah" and she's like "OMG, blah blah blah, let me guess, they're a Gemini?" And you go "Uhh . . . how did you know?" and then, all smug and snarky, they blurt out those notorious words: "Uhh, it's astrology." Well yeah, that's us. Hi! 👋 We're Ilana and Brianna, the millennial/Gen Z power duo, here to give you the only life advice you'll *ever* need.

It's V important that you understand that for us, loving astrology means blaming the stars for all our quirks and shortcomings. 💜 And we think that's healthy.

The beauty of astrology is that it reveals the magic of individuality. Think about it: the day you were born, the stars aligned in all their glory. And then, at precisely [insert time of birth] something kinda crazy happened—the planets, a.k.a. the universe, sprinkled some cosmic energy on you, and 🌸 🌸 there you were, this all-powerful babe (we picture Lady Gaga), blasted into a world of celestial chaos.

If you're new, let us be your planetary guides. Astrology is so much more than a horoscope. We don't want to argue about whether astrology is legit—we know it is! Just like the ancient star-watchers, we enjoy using astrology as a path to self-knowledge and a way to interpret our life experiences. And if you disagree, then that's cool, you're probably a Taurus or something. We'll love you anyway, because astrology embraces all.

So why should you love astrology?

1. **Discover Who You Are:** We all love a good self-analysis sesh! Do you want to know what makes you tick? Or what turns you on? Astrology's here, and she's going to delve into your secrets and reveal you to yourself.

2. **Spill the Tea:** Life is like a box of drama. You never know which catastrophe you're gonna get. Or do you? The stars can give you some hints about what's going on behind the scenes and it's sure to be spicy.

3. **Get Some Cosmic Comfort:** When you're having those "I just wanna PMS in peace" kinda days, astrology is there to validate your questionable choices.

4. **Hear Some Truth-Telling:** Astrology is honest and blunt, like your neurotic Virgo friend who always gives it to you straight.

5. And the best part—**Relationships!** What's more fascinating than figuring out your astrological compatibility? Nothing. The answer is nothing. Sharing your zodiac sign on your dating profile can provide a potential paramour with a small look into who you are and what it might be like to get to know you.

So don't sleep on the "irrelevant" pages that don't mention your sign (shoutout to Leo). You can pretty much identify yourself or someone you know on every page in this book. Is your sister like the mischievous Scorpio in the family chapter? Is your bf that emotionally unavailable Aquarius in the relationships chapter? Are YOU that crybaby Capricorn who secretly identifies as a Cancer?

You know when they say "you're not like other girls"? Well, we're not like other astrology books. And that's not just a line. This collection of illustrated astrological insights is your personal guide to friendships, relationships, situationships, familyships . . . basically all the ships. We'll explore each and every sign in their natural and not-so-natural habitats. From first dates to heartbreaks, we're here to analyze you and dish out some much-needed tough love. Relationships are hard work, and let's face it, everyone needs some cosmic intervention. Whether you're an astro-genius or just astro-curious, there's absolutely something for you here. Welcome to Astroland.

XOXO,
Ilana + Brianna

DATING

You would never get bangs without asking your friends first, so why would you date someone without consulting the cosmos? Love is unpredictable and we're earth signs, so . . . gross. Like, it's a wild time to date right now, with dating apps and D-list celebs sliding into your DMs. But there's one pickup line we can all depend on: "What's your sign?"

We're OBSESSED with this line, we honor it, we take it to an expensive dinner and NO, we don't regret the bill. 'Cause, what's dating without a little judgment?

Logically speaking, if the moon can change the tides, then we should 100 percent turn to the stars to guide our love lives. Dating is a diabolical personality puzzle, and astrology is a cheat sheet that can help us put the pieces together.

Astrology helps us commit to self-awareness so that we can better explore romantic connections with others. The purpose of this chapter is to help you find a deeper understanding of how you venture into love— your types, turn-ons, turn-offs . . . We're here to optimize your energy. Learn to embrace your mix + match cosmic qualities—attract your crush, communicate better with them, really listen to their wants, needs, dreams. Like real adult sh*t, you know?

It's time to give you all the juicy deets on what it's like to date the signs, from the deal makers to the deal breakers. Cosmic guidance *is* the best way to prejudge your date, but there are some other important things too, like—attraction, communication, and place/time, blah blah blah. Let the stars help you understand and zhuzh your connection so it works. So feel free to get a lil freaky with it.

The Signs' Dating Profiles

ARIES, ♈
Element: 🌷
"Don't hate the player, hate the game."

TAURUS, ♉
Element: 🌍
"Your parents will love me."

GEMINI, ♊
Element: ☁️
"Last time I was someone's type, I was giving blood."

CANCER, ♋
Element: 〰️
"Looking for the Ross to my Rachel. Except no breaks."

LEO, ♌
Element: 🌷
"Don't ask me when I'm free. I'm always expensive."

VIRGO, ♍
Element: 🌍
"Sophisticated spreadsheets in the streets, hot mess in the sheets."

LIBRA, ♎︎
Element: ☁️
"Buy me nice things and tell me I'm pretty."

SCORPIO, ♏︎
Element: 〰️
"I hate you. Convince me otherwise."

SAGITTARIUS, ♐︎
Element: 🔥
[Insert inspirational quote here]

CAPRICORN, ♑︎
Element: 🌐
"My time is $$$. Don't waste it."

AQUARIUS, ♒︎
Element: ☁️
"Your planet or mine?"

PISCES, ♓︎
Element: 〰️
"If you like a good documentary, I'll show you my parts unknown."

FLEXTING
a.k.a. Flirty Texting

VIRGO: What's your sign?

GEMINI: ... Trying to steal my identity? 😊

VIRGO: No, just 🖤 and maybe get a free dinner out of it too.

GEMINI: Ohhh, where are they giving out free dinners?

VIRGO: Your place.

GEMINI: ?

Okay, so can we all just agree that meeting online isn't creepy anymore? Like, we're no longer in the chatroom era and meet-cutes are so 2002. And besides, there's nothing better than the high you get from seeing "You matched" while swiping. But then comes the dreaded first text—the icebreaker. This is where most of us (calling you out, Cancer) fall short. And let's face it, a good opener makes ALL the difference.

When it comes to logical signs like Gemini and Virgo, small talk isn't gonna cut it. These signs want the CHAT, the banter, the mental mischief that gets their intellectual engines running. So don't even think about coming out the gate with a "'Sup?" Boring openers lead to boring conversations, period.

Instead, try mixing it up with a little flirty foreplay. Throw in a "Two truths and a lie," "Would you rather," or our personal favorite, "What's your sign? " 😉 You don't have to scour the internet for award-winning one-liners (although it wouldn't hurt!), but try to have some fun with it!

Confident conversations lead to connections! If you want to stand out, you gotta put in the effort. There's no perfect thing to say or magical opener to promise a response. But if you approach a conversation with empathy, confidence, and personality, you may just find that spicy sign willing to match your energy.

WHY TEXTING BLOWS,
A POEM BY EVERY WATER SIGN EVER

Left on read,
Overanalyzing emojis,
What do they mean "k"?
Words are hard,
I need a nap.

When it comes to sensitive signs like Pisces and Scorpio, intimate conversation is the key to chemistry. But sorry, texting back and forth ain't gonna cut it. Yes, Pisces will play along 'cause they're basically Care Bears, but that's not what they REALLY want. No, emotional signs like these wanna put on some Marvin Gaye and get into it—listen to your voice, study your expressions, fall in love with you after five minutes. . . 'cause that's healthy. 😳

The key to a good FaceTime chat is complete focus (and good Wi-Fi). Rid yourself of distractions, get comfortable, ask those questions you might otherwise delete before sending. Keep things casual with a friendly FaceTime, or dive deep with late-night telephone talks. All you need is half an outfit, a semi-clean room, decent lighting, and voilà: you're ready to meet your soulmate.

There's lots of reasons why opting for a virtual encounter is a good idea. For one, it allows you to vet your matches before meeting IRL. But more importantly, for the sensitive souls of the zodiac it removes the unknowns, the mind games, the anticipation of the first date. Plus, it's a great way to continue getting to know someone after you start dating. This intimate communication will allow you both to authentically vibe while giving you some space to understand your feelings and explore your options.

Amp Up the Romance

Chivalry? Dead? Not if an earth sign can help it.

Although a trip to Taco Bell and an empty parking lot might sound appealing to you *cough* Pisces *cough* Taurus will bounce at the first whiff of fast food. Tauruses have standards! So don't think about serving them mediocre cuisine unless you want to hear about it on their next podcast. Plain and simple, fancy signs like Taurus, Libra, and Leo are personally offended by minimal effort. They need some glitz and glam to get their romance revving.

While our dear Capricorns don't openly beg for soppy romance, they *do* hold their partners to a higher standard. That means no last-minute flakes and half-ass dates—hear that, Aquarius? Caps understand their worth and won't settle for Netflix and chilling (during the talking phase, at least). So whip out those red roses, open the car door—anything to ignite some fire in a Cap's cold, dead heart.

Remember, fancy romance does NOT have to break the bank. If five-star dining ain't your dish, plan a dreamy picnic under the stars. The key to having class is effort, not cash. A handwritten letter pouring out your soul will instantly spark some feelings. They'll act all grossed out, but earth signs secretly love to feel adored.

That's because they're obsessed with all things old-school. Tradition is what earthies do best! Every part of their lives is played by the books—including their romantic endeavors (If you're thinking like Gatsby, you're doing something right). And the best part about dating an earth sign? They remember *all* the little things. We're talkin' "childhood best friend's favorite color" level of detail. And they'll use that info to surprise you with the most practical and meaningful gifts. Yeah, we know, it's a lot to live up to. If ya *really* want to wow them, try purchasing a lil notepad. Attracting an earthie is like acing an exam. It takes some dedication, but it's def worth it.

So it's time to tap into that lovey-dovey personality you've repressed and stop trying to appear emotionally unavailable. A bit of romance sets the mood and creates space for deeper conversations. For the stars who expect the best, try to impress. That will go a LONG way toward setting the tone for what's to come. These special moments will build that much-needed intimacy, leading the way to true love.

Get a Little Adventurous

If you're not purchasing airline tix or taking a trapeze class, is it even a real first date? Uhhhh . . . absolutely not. Fire signs always crave an out-of-the-box adventure. So ditch the coffee shops, park walks, or bird-watching—sorry, Caps. Maybe sit this one out?

Sags need spontaneity! They'll be impressed with a surprise bonfire, ice-skating, or a (mildly) risky hike. Mount Everest is a must . . . eventually. In every area of life, a spicy Sagittarius desires someone to challenge their worldview. And what better way to do that than, uh . . . travel the world?! And while you're off globe-trotting, make sure to dive into their philosophical psyche. They have a *lot* goin' on there, and they always wanna explore their curiosity. Maybe read a book or two in preparation? We recommend this one! Have some thoughts to bring to the table. No need to be the next Shakespeare, just keep a fresh perspective.

But srsly, a Sag's open mind will take them far—on a physical and emotional level. They want to bounce opinions back and forth while climbing the Sierras, or laugh till their jaw hurts while snuggled by a campfire. Basically, you gotta be that ride or die to tag along in the game of life.

Speaking of fire, le royalty, Aries, loves to embrace their wild side. Freezing in a dark theater with a bucket of stale popcorn? No thx. Energetic activities like mini golf or laser tag will amuse their competitive side. Aries are bold, feisty, and born to succeed—so def let them win round one of *Dance Dance Revolution*. But don't go *too* easy on 'em. They need a partner who can keep up with their fast pace. So after round one . . . it's okay to show off your cha cha slide.

Oh, and please don't waste this ram's precious time. Being bored on a Saturday is a major turn-off. To reel in their rambunctious hearts, give them a reason to show up! Vibing with the same music? Time for a concert! Both love sports? Head out for a game. Make meaningful memories, and they're destined to stick around for date number two . . . unless it's a museum.

When dating fire signs, you're in for a world of passion! Shared experiences are meant to build lasting memories. From inside jokes to deep, intimate conversations, they want to know you in every scenario. So get ready, because things are about to get hot and heavy.

What turns them on the most, you say? Glad you asked . . .

TURN-ONS
for the Signs

	ADVENTUROUS	HOTNESS	MYSTERY	SUCCESS	FUNNY	IQ	SENSITIVE	ARTISTIC	ROMANTIC	KINDNESS
ARIES	X	X	X	X					X	X
TAURUS		X		X	X	X		X	X	
GEMINI	X	X	X	X	X	X				
CANCER		X			X		X	X	X	X
LEO	X	X		X	X				X	X
VIRGO		X		X	X	X		X		X
LIBRA	X	X		X		X		X		X
SCORPIO		X	X			X	X	X	X	
SAGITTARIUS	X	X		X		X		X	X	
CAPRICORN		X		X	X	X			X	X
AQUARIUS	X	X			X	X		X		X
PISCES		X			X		X	X	X	X

EARTH SIGNS (Taurus, Virgo, Capricorn): They might seem uptight, but all earthies want is a little unconditional love. They enjoy stability, consistency, and long pre-scheduled walks on the beach. So always have a plan, good hygiene, and for the love of god, BE ON TIME.

FIRE SIGNS (Aries, Leo, Sagittarius): These fighters need all the flames, so don't shy away from a romantic adventure. Fire signs know they deserve the world, which makes them a little dangerous, TBH. A stroll in the park? Instantly ghosted. Round trip to Cabo? Now you're talking.

AIR SIGNS (Gemini, Libra, Aquarius): Don't ask where they want to eat or where they want to go; they're down for whatever . . . as long as it's not boring. Stimulate these breezy babes with a little logical foreplay. So go find an art gallery or play laser tag! Keep them busy or they'll blow away.

WATER SIGNS (Cancer, Scorpio, Pisces): These H_2O hotties are all about the feels. Serenade them with sad songs, draw them a picture . . . they love that sappy, emo sh*t. Dive deep and you're destined to touch their hearts.

TURN-OFFS
for the Signs

	JEALOUSY	ARROGANCE	INSENSITIVITY	POOR HYGIENE	BORING	ARGUMENTATIVE	DRAMA	UNMOTIVATED	RESERVED	PREDICTABLE
ARIES		X	X		X			X	X	X
TAURUS		X	X	X			X	X		
GEMINI	X			X	X			X	X	X
CANCER		X	X		X	X			X	X
LEO			X	X	X			X	X	X
VIRGO			X	X	X	X	X	X		
LIBRA	X	X				X	X	X		X
SCORPIO			X	X	X			X	X	X
SAGITTARIUS		X		X	X			X	X	X
CAPRICORN	X	X	X	X			X	X		
AQUARIUS		X			X		X	X	X	X
PISCES	X	X	X		X	X		X		

When it comes to love, *every* sign has those *icks* they just can't overlook.

EARTH SIGNS (Taurus, Virgo, Capricorn): Time to get your sh*t together! These workaholics are too busy cleaning up everyone's messes to deal with your drama. So pick up all those dirty clothes before you even *think* about inviting them in. Slobs need not apply.

FIRE SIGNS (Aries, Leo, Sagittarius): These fiery optimists crave positive energy. Like, they're totally fine flying solo, so you better bring some good vibes. And don't forget to give them their freedom! Any hint of containment will extinguish their flames.

AIR SIGNS (Gemini, Libra, Aquarius): Get a hobby! Clinginess is a major ick for these independent souls. They need personal space to unplug and unwind. But when it's time to have fun, go hard or go home. Match their playful energy or you'll be blown off.

WATER SIGNS (Cancer, Scorpio, Pisces): Pack it up, Miss Know-It-All. A closed-minded egomaniac will send these H_2O hotties swimming downstream. So ditch the manipulative foreplay! Keep it real because they'll see through you like a tall glass of water.

Not-So-Good Example

Good Example

You know those first dates that are also last dates? We've all been there . . . you've never met, texting sucks, and like, nobody cares what you do for work.

Our two first-date faves: Leo + Cancer. Leo waltzes into their first encounter with the confidence of a million Instagram likes. And that can be downright intimidating. Sweet little Cancer, on the other hand, tiptoes into the date like "I'll never find love. I'm destined to be single forever." Barf.

Now look, Leo. We totally get you're the most interesting (and best-dressed) person in the room. But if you want Cancer to love you as much as you love yourself, try to actually get to know them. Ask about their hopes, dreams . . . all that water sign BS. Appeal to their imaginative, sensitive side and they'll appreciate your genuine curiosity.

Cancer, you're so sweet (and manipulative), but it's possible your obsession with romance might be clouding your judgment. Pay attention

to Leo's body language—their eye contact or intrigue level. Ask them about their accomplishments, what drives them. Get to know their passionate side before you dive in. And don't be afraid to communicate your needs—Leo will admire your honesty.

According to the cosmos, if you want a second date, you gotta adapt and find some balance. No, please don't change who you are (Pisces), 'cause the real you will attract the partner you need. Romantic preferences are confusing, so you might as well embrace your truth . . . it will come out eventually! In the meantime, step out of the spotlight, and focus on understanding your potential partner. Do you vibe with them? Are they matching your energy? Love is a tricky game, and the best way to win is being yourself (yes, we said it, get over it.)

The Signs as Kisses

sprinting to
finish line
ARIES

overly
passionate
TAURUS

battle of
the teeth
GEMINI

like their
last breath
CANCER

anywhere but
the lips
LEO

A+
Surprisingly
not bad
VIRGO

too much
tongue
LIBRA

OUCH!

accidentally
bites you
SCORPIO

tries too hard
SAGITTARIUS

efficient
CAPRICORN

eyes wide
open
AQUARIUS

#1
10/10
PISCES

To tongue or not to tongue? That is the question.

Yes, some of you signs know what you're doing (oh, hey, Scorpio), but the rest of you could use some . . . improvement. Every sign has their idea of a perfect kiss, so knowing what they like is important if you want to impress. Let's consult the cosmos . . .

EARTH SIGNS (Taurus, Virgo, Capricorn): Don't let the stereotypes fool you, earthies are sensual beings. Whisper sweet nothings in their ear while you softly sweep their lips. And please, don't forget to moisturize. These signs take kissing VERY seriously; they won't settle for sandpaper.

FIRE SIGNS (Aries, Leo, Sagittarius): Cue the fireworks! These babes expect a wild, audacious performance. Keep it playful with a little PDA. They love an audience. And don't be shy, some bottom lip biting will let them know you're in it to win it.

AIR SIGNS (Gemini, Libra, Aquarius): Think Spider-Man circa 2002. Upside down, in the rain, costumes . . . Like, you gotta keep it creative. Initiate with a little intrigue. Throw in some teasing banter—they love a little mental mouth-to-mouth.

WATER SIGNS (Cancer, Scorpio, Pisces): These sexy smoochers put wet kissing on the map. So get ready to burn some cals because you're gonna need to work that tongue. Slowly build the tension, then explode like a tidal wave. Get lost in their emotions, and they'll get lost in you.

Dating Advice

ARIES
A little planning goes a long way.

TAURUS
Step outside your comfort zone.

GEMINI
Listen to your heart, not just your mind.

CANCER
Go easy on yourself and your crushes.

LEO
Have high standards but be realistic.

VIRGO
Save the nitpicking for later.

for the Signs

LIBRA

Be ultra–communicative about where you're at and what you're looking for.

SCORPIO

Let people in once in a while and see what happens.

SAGITTARIUS

You can be honest without hurting people's feelings.

CAPRICORN

Try to loosen up a bit.

AQUARIUS

Make yourself emotionally available for once.

PISCES

Forcing intimacy won't strengthen your bond. Slow and steady FTW.

Signs You Are in a Situationship

you haven't met
their loved ones

encounters are
unplanned

superficial
conversations

you haven't had
"the talk"

SITUATIONSHIPS

If "it's complicated," "it's a thing," or you're "seeing where it goes," you're most likely in a situationship. Fun? Maybe. Confusing? Yeah.

The notorious undefined romantic relationship isn't always a bad thing. For some people (air signs!), this situation can be kinda liberating—no pressure or expectations. But for most of us (earthies!), it's important to know when it no longer serves you. It can be mentally draining to not know where you stand, wavering between the line of friendship and committed relationship, leading to anxiety, frustration, and resentment.

Situationships occur because one or both people aren't sure whether they want something more serious. Maybe the undecided partner is lonely or enjoys the pursuit. So before sticking it out, the invested partner really needs to ask themselves if this is worth fighting for (or waiting it out)? And if the answer is yes, you need to have a real honest conversation about where things are going (but we'll get to that).

No matter the outcome, use situationships as learning experiences to grow. If there were red flags, did you ignore them? What are your expectations? What do you want from dating? Really question yourself—it will help you avoid putting yourself in these confusing situations later on.

From commitment-phobe to commitment freak, will your relationship last ten years or one week?

EARTH SIGNS (Taurus, Virgo, Capricorn): If there was an award for serial monogamy, earthies would win gold, every time. Repulsed by the prospect of wasting time, these dedicated daters don't play around, and want to settle down. BUT, you better have your sh*t together, or it's game over.

FIRE SIGNS (Aries, Leo, Sagittarius): It's really hit or miss here—you either secure a life partner, or ten years of therapy. Yes, they love the chase, but they also don't mind being caught by the right relationship. Once their wandering eyes choose a path, you got a partner for life.

AIR SIGNS (Gemini, Libra, Aquarius): Inconclusive and impulsive, these weirdos have some major issues in the commitment department. If the vibe is (slightly) off, they float up, up, and away. These signs change more than you before a first date.

WATER SIGNS (Cancer, Scorpio, Pisces): Buckle up, you're in it for the long haul. Now enjoy the emotional roller coaster. These emo signs tend to dwell in the dating phase, where passion runs high, and dedication remains distant. But once they decide their feelings are real, they're all in.

First Hook-Up
Well, that happened. Hehehe.
OMG that happened . . . what am I supposed to feel?
Yeah, that was fun!
I'm hungry.

6 Months In

This feels like it's getting serious. Should I say something?
Ugh, I'm SO in love. But I don't wanna make them uncomfortable . . .
I'm so glad things haven't gotten weird between us.
Why would it be weird? We're friends.

So you had a little too much fun last night and you accidentally slipped into your friend's bed because your life is basically a '90s sitcom. Oops? Yes, you always thought your friend was cute, but you're not so sure there's romance there. How are you supposed to stay friends with someone after you've seen them naked?

Enter two signs that constantly find themselves in a friends with benefits (FWB) situationship: Pisces and Aquarius.

Pisces is soooo dreamy. You might think they're an unlikely choice for FWB, but their water sign ways actually allow them to go with the flow, pretty effortlessly—cool, collected, and always DTF (down to flirt . . . get your mind out of the gutter).

The love addict that they are, Pisces will often blur the lines between FWB and hot and heavy romance, but they know how to play by the rules. Their free-flowing ways appeal to someone like Aqua, who dreads labels. But Pisces needs to be honest with themselves. If on the inside they're screaming "WHAT ARE WE?" they should probably set some boundaries instead of diving too deep or swimming away.

Our little social butterflies, Aquarius is incredibly popular, with a packed calendar. It takes a lot for them to settle down in a real relationship, so they often opt for the pressure-free FWB. Aqua loves connecting on an emotional level, so this casual dynamic is the perfect situation. They get to vibe with someone they genuinely care about, while still maintaining their personal freedom.

Aqua can sense when things are getting a little too serious for their liking. Like, once hand holding enters the equation, you've officially entered relationship territory to them. It's important for Aqua to be direct about where they're at.

No matter your sign, when it comes to FWBs, focus on preserving the "F" before the "B." Whatever feels right for you and your "buddy" is what you should pursue. But set some ground rules—things can get tricky real fast, especially when feelings get involved. Be sure to have open communication and mutual respect. THOSE are benefits worth preserving. Good luck!

Virtual Situationships

IT'S A MATCH!

CAPRICORN, ♑
Element: 🌍
"My time is $$$.
Don't waste it."

SAGITTARIUS, ♐
Element: 🔥
[Insert inspirational
quote here]

DAY 1:

♑ Hey 🤍 you have a typo in your bio.

I SO do not... ♐

♑ It says you're single 😉

Are you trying to change that? ♐

♑ I WILL change that.

We'll see... ♐

DAY 7:

Hey baby, what's shaking? ♐

♑ Just working, wyd?

Just landed in Fiji.
Wanna FaceTime? 😜 ♐

♑ Sure, let's schedule it!
What's your calendar look like?

...calendar? 🤨 ♐

DAY 14:

♑ Sorry, work's been crazy, but I do want to hang.

♐ Yah, totally! I'm free after pottery class.

♑ Yes, let's do it — I can be spontaneous?

(3 hours later)

♐ Sorry! The pilot said to turn our phones off before takeoff.

♑ ...Wait, where are you?

---

1 MONTH:

♑ I think we should meet—to see if this is worth both our time.

♐ Sure! That sounds fun

♑ I just want to figure out what this is and if it's a forever thing.

♐ But nothing is forever! ♐

♑ ...

Aww, the digital love story. Once you hope for their name to pop up in every notification, you know you caught the feels. It starts with an innocent swipe or a DM, and ends up taking up 95 percent of your headspace. And the best part: you've never met IRL. No clue what the physical chemistry is like. Just pics, messages, video chats, and following each other on social media.

This is the reality of the modern day virtual situationship—exhausting, thrilling, unpredictable, and most of the time, it peters out into nothingness. Unless you take the time to *really* nurture it and make plans to *eventually* meet up. No, not in that creepy "I met a stranger on the internet way." More like, virtual besties turned lovers?

When it comes to virtual situationships, Capricorn absolutely thrives. This is their time to shine. A creature of habit, Capricorn will stay consistent with good-morning texts and regular FaceTime calls. They love the planning, scheduling, and avoidance of spontaneity.

However, if the virtual energy is not being reciprocated, they're the first to flee. Cap only puts their effort where they know a reward is waiting (a.k.a. a meaningful friendship/relationship). So if the vibe is off, they will happily spread their love elsewhere.

Meanwhile, our freedom-loving Sag enjoys the open space created by an online situationship. The constant threat of solid, in-person plans completely disrupts their go-with-the-flow attitude.

Like Cap, Sagittarius prefers being in charge of their own time, and will remain inconsistently consistent with calls, texts, and FaceTime. Like, one night they may call you at 3:00 a.m. while sitting on an eerily dark sidewalk, the next day they're texting you about their impromptu trip to Bali. 'Cause it's Sag's world and we're all just here. And Cap enjoys the controlled exposure to chaos.

Both of these liberated signs relish the freedom that comes with staying virtual. But this is only a transitional phase. Eventually, they'll both want to "figure things out" (a.k.a. put a label on the relationship). And that requires meeting up, feeling out each other's energy, and of course, "the talk" (dun dun dun).

"THE TALK"

Initiates	Avoids
VIRGO	PISCES
TAURUS	SAGITTARIUS
CAPRICORN	LIBRA
ARIES	CANCER
SCORPIO	AQUARIUS
LEO	GEMINI

TIPS FOR HAVING "THE TALK":

1. Choose the right time to have the conversation, after you've been steadily seeing each other for a while.
2. Have the conversation in person, in a quiet, private place.
3. Don't be afraid! Remind yourself it's okay to ask for what you want.
4. Don't blindside them. Ease into the conversation.
5. Let them know if you're nervous.
6. Keep it simple, straightforward, and honest.
7. Don't put too much pressure on yourself to find the perfect words.
8. Give the other person time to think it over.
9. Don't worry if it doesn't go the way you'd hoped.
10. End the convo with a decision: either walk away or wait it out.

Most Likely to GHOST

Key: ★ = companion for life
★★★★★ = serial ghoster

VIRGO ★★★★   PISCES ★★★
TAURUS ★   SAGITTARIUS ★★★★★
CAPRICORN ★★   LIBRA ★★★★
ARIES ★★★   CANCER ★★
SCORPIO ★★   AQUARIUS ★★★★★
LEO ★★★   GEMINI ★★★★★

Ghosting, also known as icing or simmering, is when the person you've been chatting with disappears without warning. And then, they ignore you, which is cute, except not. So which signs do it best? Let's discuss . . .

♈ **ARIES:** If you've been ghosted by a dedicated ram, it's definitely personal. Aries will fight for a bond that meets their needs. If they feel unfulfilled, they'll simply set their sights elsewhere, and vanish without a trace. This one might sting a little, 'cause they seem so devoted . . . until they leave.

♉ **TAURUS:** Guided by an impeccable moral compass, Taurus rarely ghosts, and if they do, it's for good reason. They face life head-on, and that means being up front about where they stand in a relationship. Even if they're tempted to give the ghost, their logical mind always wins, and they'll opt for a kindly written text.

♊ **GEMINI:** You already knew this one was coming. The thesaurus deems Gemini a synonym for ghosting, because one moment they're sending you mixed signals, and the next day, no more signals. Poof. Gone. But don't worry, they'll be back, texting you at 12:00 a.m. to let you know they had a dream about you.

♋ **CANCER:** These gentle souls enter your life like a drop of rain— and evaporate just as quickly. Once things get too serious, they'll disappear without a trace. Cancer fears feeling pain and betrayal, so they avoid situations that feel like they'll end in heartbreak. It's okay, Cancer, we understand where you're coming from. And we feel you.

♌ **LEO:** These fiery spirits love the passion that tags along with a fresh fling. In fact, they live for it. It's like being the main character in their own reality show. But once the initial spark fades, they either settle down, or drift away. So it's not *really* ghosting.

♍ **VIRGO:** Yes, the rumors are true. Virgos are super committed. But don't be fooled: it takes them a long time, and plenty of deep introspection, to arrive at this place. You gotta ease 'em into the relationship. The first scent of pressure, and Virgo will happily slam the door in your face. No regrets.

♎ **LIBRA:** This one's a little confusing because Libra loves a healthy relationship. But they struggle to understand that conflict is inherent in communication. So if they sense discomfort too early on, they might possibly run for the hills. And there's no coming back, like ever.

♏ **SCORPIO:** Once you get past that nasty stinger, Scorpio quickly devotes themselves to a budding relationship. They won't even consider dating someone without long-term potential, so it's unlikely they'll ghost you out of the blue. And if they do, it isn't personal. They're probably just too overwhelmed.

♐ **SAGITTARIUS:** These wanderlusters go hardcore in a new relationship. This makes the letdown even more painful. 'Cause once Sag sees past their romanticized vision of the situation, they'll def be re-signing up for every single dating app. And updating their profile with the pics you took of them, btw.

♑ **CAPRICORN:** No, Cap won't ghost you. But they'll def hurt your feelings. They want to respect your time (and theirs), so they'll send you an expertly composed goodbye text (or email) once they decide to leave, like a flipped switch. And once a Cap makes their grand exit, you're never (ever) getting back together.

♒ **AQUARIUS:** That detached and mysterious vibe is so alluring, until Aqua stops answering your calls, won't return your texts, and six months later, posts about their self-discovery journey across the globe. Their personal agenda comes first, even if the chemistry is there. So unless you're *the one*, they'll move on.

♓ **PISCES:** It's not that they don't like you. They do. They really do. It's just . . . commitment is so scary. And life is so short. And relationships are hard. So yeah, they'll ghost you. But they'll still think about you a lot, if that's any consolation. And don't worry, Pisces will definitely slide back into your DMs in three to six months, just to say "hey."

SITUATIONSHIPS

PROS

no responsibility

pressure-free

thrill of the chase

no awkward social responsibilities

easy to exit

CONS

no commitment

potentially ruining
a friendship

draining on
your emotions

lots of
uncertainty
= anxiety

no plans
for a
future

Compatibility Chart

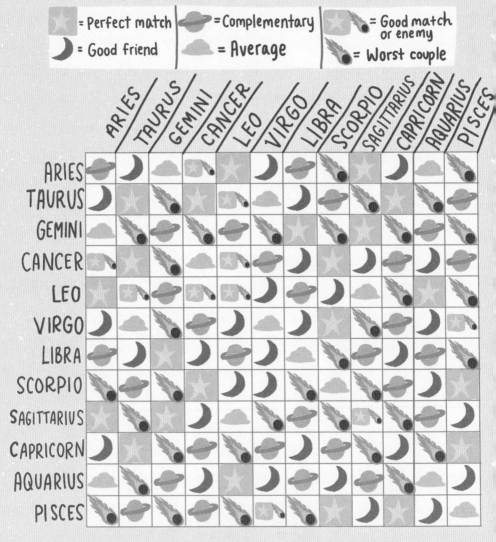

RELATIONSHIPS

The chapter you've ALLLL been waiting for is here! Because admit it, taking control of your romantic destiny sounds downright delicious. (Right, Taurus?)

But before we dive in, let's start with this much-needed disclaimer: astrological compatibility is complex. Just because two signs are deemed *incompatible*, doesn't mean they can't make it work. Look at Will and Jada (Libra + Virgo), a classic coupling. On the flipside, just because you're a *perfect* match doesn't mean you're meant to last. RIP Kim and Kanye (Libra + Gemini).

We're not here to tell you whether it's in the stars or just in your head. Like, we're not psychics. But we *are* here to give you the insight you need to power your relationship. Remember, ALL relationships require love, respect, and a mutual love of canceling plans because you hate everyone. But they also require a deeper understanding of the person you're with— what are their wants, needs, turns-ons, pet peeves? How do they communicate and how do they fornicate? It's time to spill the astrological tea . . .

Libras are the true masters of balance. But when it comes to the HM phase, all bets are off. Libra wants the kind of romance you see in the movies—butterflies, sparkly gifts, and endless compliments. In their eyes, this energy sets the tone for the entire relationship. But beware, Libra fears complacency, so give them a little freedom along the way, to keep the mystery alive.

As for our astute Aquas, the HM phase is *anything* but superficial—it's a time to explore the hidden corners of their lover's mind. Make sure to reciprocate that curious energy by asking lots of hard-hitting questions. Aquas wanna get straight to the heart of things. Once that magical spark begins to fade, it's important to keep up the momentum.

These signs need lots of space to breathe (hello, they *are* air), so the HM phase is the time to secure that connection. They share a mutual interest in exploring the beauty of the world and therefore, one another. But although they might have elevated IQs, they struggle to wean off the high of the HM phase. So getting past this period is crucial! Once they do, they'll have partners for life.

Love Languages

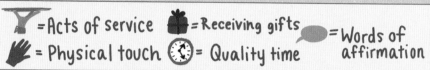

🍸 = Acts of service 🎁 = Receiving gifts 💬 = Words of affirmation
✋ = Physical touch 🕐 = Quality time

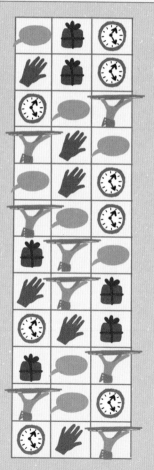

ARIES	Words of affirmation	Receiving gifts	Quality time
TAURUS	Physical touch	Receiving gifts	Quality time
GEMINI	Quality time	Words of affirmation	Acts of service
CANCER	Acts of service	Physical touch	Words of affirmation
LEO	Words of affirmation	Physical touch	Quality time
VIRGO	Acts of service		Quality time
LIBRA	Receiving gifts	Acts of service	Words of affirmation
SCORPIO	Physical touch	Acts of service	Receiving gifts
SAGITTARIUS	Quality time	Physical touch	Receiving gifts
CAPRICORN	Receiving gifts	Words of affirmation	Acts of service
AQUARIUS	Acts of service	Words of affirmation	Quality time
PISCES	Quality time	Physical touch	Acts of service

If you haven't heard of *The Five Love Languages* by Gary Chapman, you've clearly been living under a rock. Thank goodness we're here to educate you.

So what can your zodiac sign tell you about your love language? Um . . . a lot.

From Scorpio's delicious physical touches to Leo's extravagant words of affirmation, each sign has their own not-so-secret recipe for love. Remember that we tend to give the way we want to receive, so taking a look at how we express ourselves is a good way to tell what our love language is.

If you're not in a relationship at the moment, take this time to study up on what the signs deem acceptable in a romantic entanglement. Read it all. Now read it again. Knowing this information will help you define the type of relationship that will bring you the most joy.

Now if you are in a relationship, be extra sure to read our little love language guide! Maybe it'll shine some light on why you and your SO squabble and how to navigate that. Or maybe it'll reaffirm what you need in a relationship so you can let your partner in on the fun. Remember, communication is key and we're not gonna stop lecturing you about it.

Communication Is Key

Relationships aren't complicated, sweetie, *people* are.

Communication is key for a healthy relationship, especially with Leo and Gemini. Leo, ruled by vitality and self-expression, may have a bit of a one-sided view of their relationship. But it's not (always) selfish. They're just super confident and want things to be like T. Swift's "Love Story."

If you're perceptive enough, you'll be able to see past Leo's alpha exterior. This sign is highly sensitive, passionate, and treats love like a battlefield. They will hide behind their ego at all costs 'cause they don't want to seem needy, but let's be honest . . . they're more readable than you on your period. So what's a Gem to do?

Gemini is ALLLL about communication—they're literally ruled by it. The only drama Gemini wants is in the boudoir, thank you very much. This sign dislikes conflict and will walk away before things get too heated. These astute litigators can easily go around an argument, so attacking them might not be the best option. They'll do whatever it takes to defend their honor. So you better have your facts and figures straight. Childish antics won't get you anywhere.

Signs like Leo can be super frustrating because Gemini demands respect in a relationship. So instead of speaking to Gem like they're a member of your studio audience, Leo needs to hop off the stage and have some healthy one-on-one time. Talk your issues out respectfully and LOGICALLY. It will work wonders for your relationship.

Gemini and Leo can be a match made in heaven, but they'll require AI communication. Gemini, the master of receipts, will sit down and talk sh*t out, point blank. This directness may annoy Leo. Like, it may turn them on, but their ego doesn't like it. Gem's gotta remain calm and collected when approaching their Leo partner. If not, well, don't say we didn't warn you . . .

And if talking out loud is overwhelming, try writing down your feelings! Gem doesn't mind a lengthy email, handwritten note, or a ten-minute audio message that restarts from the beginning every three seconds. As long as you externalize your emotions, they'll appreciate it.

The Signs in Bed

action-packed
ARIES

slow +
irresistible
TAURUS

dirty
talkers
GEMINI

intuitive +
loving
CANCER

flaunting
their goods
LEO

calculated
to perfection
VIRGO

all about the
aesthetics
LIBRA

fun with
fetishes
SCORPIO

always an
adventure
SAGITTARIUS

Old
Hollywood-esque
CAPRICORN

other-
worldly
AQUARIUS

hypnotic
bliss
PISCES

Speaking of the sack . . . let's transition from the streets to the sheets. You ready for this?

EARTH SIGNS (Capricorn, Taurus, Virgo): Work hard, play hard. That's basically all you need to know. There's no such thing as a quickie for a sensual and romantic earthie. Take your time, use your hands effectively, and for the love of God, *please* wash your junk. Earthies like their partners fresh!

FIRE SIGNS (Aries, Sagittarius, Leo): The Black Eyed Peas achieved the unthinkable by releasing "Boom Boom Pow" in 2009. It's a straight-up guide for sex with a fire sign. Expect dramatic flairs, intense glares, and lots of theatrics.

AIR SIGNS (Libra, Gemini, Aquarius): Gettin' frisky with an air sign will transport you to another planet. These super-sensual creatures will rock your world, serving the sexy talk and lusty lingerie. Scintillating foreplay is an absolute must. After all, it's the journey, not the destination!

WATER SIGNS (Scorpio, Cancer, Pisces): When it comes to sexy time, our agua cuties unleash their deepest fantasies . . . and they have *a lot* of 'em. There's also a 99 percent chance they'll end up crying for some reason. Just bring tissues. You'll need those either way, TBH.

You know that cringy couple that basically lives on their couch, draped over each other like koala bears? Yeah, that's a Virgo/Pisces pairing. And we're all a little jealous. That's 'cause these two lovebirds have a magnetic connection that's off the charts. And here's why: they're opposing signs, meaning they were born six months apart. And we all know that opposites attract.

Virgo and Pisces productively evolve together. One year into their relationship, and they both seem like completely different people. But these two hold an intense emotional connection. They both live to serve and support each other.

Known as the sign of well-being, Virgos love to holistically take care of their partner. They give practically, often with acts of service—cleaning your home, watering your plants, introducing you to proper hygiene. This earthie will invest in you like a 401k, steadily and over time. But, like, Virgo is a bit uptight. No, like, the most uptight sign in the zodiac. Luckily, Pisces helps Virgo let their guard down. They'll be reluctant at first (no one tells Virgo what to do) but will eventually cave. Pisces is one of the only signs that makes Virgo feel understood and relaxed. And let's face it Virgo, you *can* be super stubborn. We get that you like to keep it real and yes, no one does it like you do, but you gotta live in the moment sometimes, ya know?

Pisces, you're just the cutest. Like, you're so nice. You're literally the zodiac sign of unconditional love. All you want to do is please and support your partner. And we love that for you. But you kind of get lost a lot. We adore your bright imagination, but you gotta actually put your dreams to work. Virgo will push you to be an actual adult. So once you two are happily paired off, don't be surprised if you wake up earlier, go to the gym, religiously drink celery juice, and commit yourself to an intriguing career. Pisces admires Virgo's intellect and welcomes their advice. And Pisces, when you're successful, you're electric. Rihanna, much?

Virgo + Pisces is a magical pairing where growth is inevitable. Virgo calms down and becomes more affectionate, exploring their romantic and sensual side. Pisces ditches their Eeyore persona and revs up their ambition, learning to be more organized, driven, and detail oriented. Plus, they'll have glowing skin because Virgo will buy them all the best face masks and night creams.

These two complement each other so well it makes us swoon, but they're not without conflict. While we love a good water-earth combo, they're still opposing signs, so they can run into some issues. In order to have a healthy relationship where they can grow, they'll both need to feel secure and confident enough to be real with one another. And they gotta learn to lean in and adapt to their partner's differences too. If they can do that, we dare say they're the most compatible couple in the cosmos. And that's a fact.

How to Keep the LDR Romance Alive

sharing your
location
ARIES

order them
Postmates
TAURUS

8-hour
phone convos
GEMINI

Sending
TikToks
CANCER

IG Stories
shoutouts
LEO

handwritten
letters
VIRGO

texts only
please
LIBRA

steamy
FaceTime session
SCORPIO

share a journal
together
SAGITTARIUS

daily email
updates
CAPRICORN

movie streaming
dates
AQUARIUS

sending
sexy pics
PISCES

EARTH SIGNS (Capricorn, Taurus, Virgo): Our earthies need some space, even in an LDR. Random acts of kindness will keep that connection alive—so send them a dozen roses, a yummy Postmates, or even a virtual hug. (So cringe. But *so* cute.)

FIRE SIGNS (Aries, Sagittarius, Leo): This flame needs constant fuel to stay alive, especially when distance is added to the equation. Consistent updates and social media shout-outs are a must. Your love deserves to be celebrated!

AIR SIGNS (Libra, Gemini, Aquarius): If you temporarily ghost an air sign, they'll prob just assume you're cheating. Or in a ditch somewhere. Soothe their senses with some flirty texts throughout the day, and always keep a FT date on the sched!

WATER SIGNS (Scorpio, Cancer, Pisces): Our emotional H_2O crave regular intimacy, despite the distance. Don't be afraid to amp up the (virtual) steam. Reminder: *don't* include your face in any pics. You don't need future employers to see all that bod.

Relationship Boundaries

Ah, boundaries. The unknown. A delicate balance between intimacy and privacy. We all have 'em, we all need 'em, and we all blatantly ignore them. Until now.

Boundaries are super essential for any healthy relationship. But they frighten the signs. And they shouldn't. They are NOT brick walls meant to keep your partner out, rather they're a set of expectations, ranging from honesty to space for independence and respect for each other's emotions.

Scorpio + Cancer really struggles in the boundaries department. Scorp's tsunami of emotions *sometimes* overwhelms the rational part of their brain that says "Maybe I shouldn't be snooping on my partner's phone at 3:00 a.m." And yeah it's hard to resist that urge, especially when their passcode is your anniversary date. *It's like an invitation.* Or not. Romantic partners are entitled to their privacy too.

Due to their need for power, Scorpio has their walls up. They like to control what they share with their SO and avoid conflict at all costs. Instead, they stew, letting their jealousy marinate like fine arsenic. For a successful relationship, there needs to be a bit more fluidity. No, Scorpio doesn't have to bulldoze their walls down overnight, but a subtle chipping away would be nice. It's all about ~balance~.

Cancer, on the other hand, often fails to speak up. They understand their personal boundaries, but struggle with enforcing them. That people-pleasing mindset does them NO favors. Cancer would rather be disappointed in themselves, than let down someone else.

Newsflash, Cancer: if your partner leaves you for establishing a boundary, then it was so *not* meant to be. Instead, be deliberate when setting standards and asking for support. Find ways to intentionally give back. After finding a middle ground, your relationship will flourish.

Scorpio + Cancer is a great pair but when it comes to boundaries, they need a lil work. To avoid conflict, both water signs have a hidden superpower: an *extremely* intelligent and rational mind. Who woulda thought? If they listen to the voice of reason, and find that balance, all boundaries will fall into place. And they'll be the obnoxious rom-com you'll hate to love.

Phases of Relationships

PHASE 1: HONEYMOON

PHASE 2:
REALITY

So, takeout again?

Omg yes.

PHASE 3:
FIGHT OR FLIGHT

Relationships are kind of like algebra. Have you ever looked at X and been like . . . Y?

Here's our philosophy: relationships have five phases.

The Honeymoon Phase: Time to merge, y'all! Yes, we covered this already, but let's sum it up! The first stage of a relationship is the initial BOOM: a passionate, sizzling romance that consumes you, also known as infatuation. You're insatiable, spending your days naked in the bedroom, enjoying your bubble, boundaries forgotten. This emotional stage is not rational, but it's fun. And if you enjoy all those pleasant chemicals—dopamine, oxytocin, endorphins—you'll adore this addictive phase . . . while it lasts.

The Reality Phase: Time to wake up from that delightful dream, because reality is here and she's a real b*tch. Now you're becoming WAY more aware of your SO and who they really are. It's time to figure out if you wanna move forward with this relationship long term and deepen your connection. This stage comes and goes more than Pisces with their ex, so be prepared.

The Fight or Flight Phase: Because we're all different and kind of annoying TBH, sh*t's bound to hit the fan. Power struggles are a very real and natural part of any entanglement. Your partner may start to irritate you, you'll wonder whether they're perfect enough (stop overthinking, Virgo). At this point, you're going to have to flex those conflict management skills you learned in fourth grade. Face your relationship problems head-on and TALK. IT. OUT. Once you deal, you'll learn the lessons you need to be the best for each other. Pro tip: love languages come in handy here.

The Nesting Phase: Okay, so now you can finally relax. Your SO and you have decided that this relationship is worth building on. This is also known as the comfortable phase. Unlike the Fight or Flight Phase, where you secretly have a little anxiety about whether you want to continue, this phase is where you've sort of decided this is something you want to stick out. And yeah, this phase may seem boring for some *Sorry, Aries*, but it's REALLY not. In fact, it's essential for a long-term match. We ALL need those nights spent lounging on the couch. And if you need a tutorial, Taurus is available.

The True Love Phase: Well, you did it! Graduation day has arrived. Your relationship is at its healthiest and you're feeling this spiritual, unconditional love. You're finally starting to accept your partner's imperfections *well not you, Cap, but that's cool* and feel more secure in your relationship. You appreciate your partner for who they are and what they bring into your life. And you feel like you've met your match. How precious.

But remember this: these phases are recurrent, NOT sequential. Just because you reach Phase 5, doesn't mean you won't revisit Phase 1. Every stage gets explored and re-explored at some point or another. Relationships change because life, circumstances, and people change! So it's totally normal for our astro couples to experience some ups and downs. And yes, you two still have A LOT of work to do, but you'll be fine because you'll do it together, and well, love conquers ALL or whatever, right?

FAMOUS DUOS

♊ GEMINI   ♊ GEMINI

David Burtka +
Neil Patrick Harris

♋ CANCER

♏ SCORPIO

Tom Hanks +
Rita Wilson

♐ SAG

♎ LIBRA

Cardi B +
Offset

Tips to Get through a Breakup

KEEP YOURSELF BUSY WITH FAMILY, FRIENDS, AND ACTIVITIES.

TREAT YOURSELF TO SELF-CARE NIGHTS.

MOVE YOUR BODY EVERY DAY (YOGA, WALKS, ETC.).

SET FIRM BOUNDARIES TO LIMIT CONTACT.

WRITE YOUR FEELINGS IN A JOURNAL.

PROCESS FEELINGS OUT LOUD.

WATCH YOUR FAVE COMFORT SHOW OR START A NEW SHOW.

HEARTBREAK AND HEALING ✴

You know that euphoric, intoxicating high you experience when you get into a new relationship? That yummy, electric, addictive feeling that makes your whole body tingle? Yeah, breakups are the opposite of that. They're quite literally THE WORST. Losing a relationship is tough no matter the situation.

How you deal with a breakup has to do with SO many factors—how close you were, if you've experienced heartbreak before, how much self-love you practice, what sign you are . . .

Looking to the cosmos for how your sign approaches these challenges can be quite insightful when it comes to matters of the heart, and it can help you learn some valuable coping skills. After all, we each experience intense emotions when dealing with a breakup—from sadness (water signs) to anger (fire signs) or even rejection (earth signs). Or maybe you feel relieved (air signs), and that's okay too.

Read on to learn how your sign and others approach breakups, how they handle the fallout, and how they heal. And don't forget, no matter your sign, you can get through anything, and we mean that.

The Signs as Breakup Lines

"There's no spark between us."
ARIES

"It's not me, it's you."
TAURUS

"This isn't stimulating me anymore."
GEMINI

"I still love you, but I can't be with you."
CANCER

"I don't see a future here."
LEO

"I need time to work on myself."
VIRGO

"I'm just not ready."
LIBRA

"We just want different things."
SCORPIO

"I'm just not in the place to commit right now."
SAGITTARIUS

"It appears you've stopped trying."
CAPRICORN

"I think we're better off as friends."
AQUARIUS

"You deserve better."
PISCES

Sometimes things don't last and it's time to bid adieu . . . So how do the signs end it?

EARTH SIGNS (Taurus, Virgo, Capricorn): Let's talk logistics. No, but seriously, earthies are going to explain very clearly why you're no longer a suitable match. Calm, and somewhat removed, they might share their pros and cons list with you—don't be surprised. And no, they won't be back.

FIRE SIGNS (Aries, Leo, Sagittarius): These fiery babes blaze through breakups—they are short, sweet, and to the damn point. They don't want to waste their time having a long, arduous conversation. So they'll give it to you straight—like ripping off a Band-Aid. And yes, it's going to hurt.

AIR SIGNS (Gemini, Libra, Aquarius): Take some pre-workout supplements 'cause you're in for quite the marathon. It's gonna feel like you're on trial, so prepare for a long-winded debate. These signs want you to understand every reason why the relationship is over. Good luck!

WATER SIGNS (Cancer, Scorpio, Pisces): Bust out the Neosporin because these breakups are gonna leave a mark . . . most likely a gaping, emotional wound. There're gonna be tears and probably a hot make-out sesh. Frankly, it's all very confusing and feels unfinished . . .

How the Signs Handle a Breakup

CANCER

Breaking up is a pretty universal experience that will most likely always suck. But remember, when it comes to broken love, good things fall apart to make room for better things to come together.

Such is the case with Cancer + Virgo. A pretty great duo TBH, but as with any couple, things get shaky due to poor communication, lack of trust, or simply, bad timing.

Cancers use their crabby shells to protect themselves. Losing someone they felt safe with is going to be rough, but don't worry, they have their process. They'll start by cutting off contact to establish firm boundaries. Then, once they've watched *The Notebook* for the one hundredth time, they'll call their friends to come over and comfort them. Cancer needs A LOT of time to heal and mend, so if you're their bestie, block out your calendar. And yeah, Cancer is pretty graceful about their breakups, but don't be surprised if they burn their ex's sh*t. Remembering the past is so unnecessary.

Meanwhile, Virgo is having quite the productive breakup. They don't want to deal with the emotions that come with dramatic life events, so they focus on what they can control, like work or their skincare routine. You can always tell when a Virgo gets dumped because they'll have endless convos with their bestie, analyzing their *seemingly perfect* ex and every reason possible that it ended (which Virgo believes is their doing, obviously). It would suit Virgo to get real—your partner wasn't perfect, at least not for you, so take them off that pedestal. You're better than that.

The truth is, Virgo and Cancer aren't really that different when it comes to breakups. Both these signs see their relationships through a rigid scope of romanticism, so they're likely to have a pretty difficult breakup. Virgo will go on their merry way, pretending everything is okay, probably buying more houseplants to fill the void, while Cancer will drown their sorrows in poetry or songwriting. Both need to process their emotions slowly and steadily, with lots of space from one another so they have time to heal.

Some signs try to avoid their heartbreak, while others post depressing, ominous quotes to their socials. Some quickly jump into bed with a new lover, while others take time to heal and fly solo. No matter your cosmic style, it's important to reflect on your breakup—what went wrong and what could improve next time? What did you learn from your previous relationship and how can you grow from it? Don't forget that breakups are life lessons, not punishments—AND you're going to be okay!

How the Signs Get Over Breakups

SAD LOVE SONGS
ON REPEAT

ARIES

THE SECRET
SPY

TAURUS

SELF-LOVE
LEADER

GEMINI

THE COUCH
DWELLER

CANCER

SOCIAL MEDIA
JUNKIE

LEO

THE BUSY
BEE

VIRGO

THE LATE-NIGHT
DRIVER

LIBRA

NEW HAIR,
WHO DIS?

SCORPIO

THE REBOUND
BABE

SAGITTARIUS

HIDE THE
MEMORIES

THE BINGE-
WATCHER

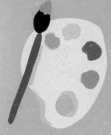

THE PASSION
PROJECT

CAPRICORN   AQUARIUS   PISCES

They say the only way to get over it is to get under it. That's simply not the case. Each sign has their own (unique) coping mechanisms to heal from a breakup.

♈ **Aries:** Not a fan of public humiliation, Aries will take this time to sulk . . . by themselves. They view a breakup as an epic fail—and would rather take this L in peace, dwelling in their heartbreak playlist.

♉ **Taurus:** This earthie needs answers . . . like yesterday. We're not saying this is healthy, but Taurus will turn into a literal FBI agent and dissect their ex's every last word.

♊ **Gemini:** A breakup is a Gemini's personal *Reputation* era (Swifties know what's up!). This is a Gem's time to become a plant mother, use that SoulCycle membership, and overall, become an upgraded version of themselves.

♋ **Cancer:** Miss Drama did not come to play. Cue the soppy rom-coms, tear-soaked pillows, and dusty Cheetos fingers. It's okay, Cancer, we've all been there.

♌ **Leo:** No time to grieve if you up and leave! That's the Leo way. A tightly packed social calendar is the only way to cope (or not cope?) with a breakup.

♍ **Virgo:** Yeah, Virgo may be dying inside. But their social media says otherwise! And this strategy kinda works . . . in a "fake it till you make it" type of way.

♎︎ **Libra:** Was that a hyena? Or a Libra screaming their hearts out while coasting down the highway at 3:00 a.m.? Either way, we're frightened. But supportive, nonetheless.

♏︎ **Scorpio:** A fresh new cut basically heals the heartbreak. Who can focus on emotions with uneven bangs poking your eyes? Scorpio picks up the shears, and never looks back. Bold moves ONLY (please call your stylist).

♐︎ **Sagittarius:** The farther away, the better. Sag prefers to rebound in an exotic location, to truly gain a fresh perspective on what went wrong in the relationship. Self-reflection is just easier while sipping on a piña colada.

♑︎ **Capricorn:** Avoidance is EVERYTHING for this perfectionist. Why feel your feelings when you can just . . . self-isolate and drown yourself in your work? It's such a simple concept.

♒︎ **Aquarius:** Brain: off. Television: on. Lights: down. Feet: up. This is the only answer for Aquarius, who's hell-bent on repressing every memory. Until they find themselves on the bathroom floor of the club at 2:00 a.m., wondering where it all went wrong . . .

♓︎ **Pisces:** Our creative Pisces channels that pain into something beautiful. They deeply process their emotions, produce a magical piece of art, and go along their merry way. (Yes, we all strive to be Pisces.)

How to Date Yourself

EARTH SIGNS (Taurus, Virgo, Capricorn): Sensory overload dominates an earth sign's existence. Like, they are super in tune with the universe, often to their own detriment. Meditation + lavender diffusers + cute plants = a much-needed escape from the overwhelming chaos of life.

FIRE SIGNS (Aries, Leo, Sagittarius): TBH, it must be exhausting to be so hot all the time. Fire signs need to calm those flames, and rock a whole day of pure duvet. This relaxing break allows our feisty babes to connect with suppressed emotions and desires.

AIR SIGNS (Gemini, Libra, Aquarius): Sometimes running away from your problems isn't really that bad of an idea. For our airy spirits, a solo adventure provides the ideal opportunity to re-engage with their identity and find some inner peace.

WATER SIGNS (Cancer, Scorpio, Pisces): Get a little wild and connect with that inner child. From hiking to gardens and leisurely afternoon strolls, water signs thrive in a wholesome and natural environment. It reinvigorates their sense of wonder, which can sometimes be quashed after a draining relationship.

Self-Love Horoscope

♈ **Aries:** Bold, tenacious, unstoppable. Since you put your heart and soul into everything work-related and glow from a good adoration sesh, you should channel some of that fiery energy into a passion project. You thrive when you visualize your goals. And we know you've got a lot.

♉ **Taurus:** Dedicated, enduring, strong. You've got it all . . . almost. Taur, you're kind of prone to relaxing a little too much, so try to move your body more. A nature walk is the perfect way for you to honor your body while taking in Mother Earth, a force that grounds you, right?

♊ **Gemini:** Versatile, intelligent, lively. We know you love to communicate but sometimes too much chat can drain your social battery. So take a break with some much-needed alone time. Oh, and throw some yoga or meditation in there too, 'cause you'll be bored without it.

♋ **Cancer:** Intuitive, caring, imaginative. You do have a way with words, but when you're revved up, you don't always come across so hot. So why not journal your feelings away? This is a great way to reflect on your emotions so you can thoughtfully express that huge heart of yours.

♌ **Leo:** Joyful, enigmatic, loyal. You're always on the go, Leo, but isn't it a bit exhausting after a while? Instead, retreat with some fabulous at-home self-care—face masks, bubble baths, a mani-pedi. FOMO is so NOT a big deal. You'll be fine.

♍ **Virgo:** Detail-oriented, reliable, creative. You're always there for everyone else, but not so much for yourself. Time for a solo outing. Take yourself to dinner, a movie, and finish the night with a little self-love. Heaven knows you need it and yeah, you deserve it.

♎ **Libra:** Charming, conciliatory, affectionate. You're always there to save the day and resolve a crisis, but when do you have time to ponder your own issues? Set the introspective mood with a clean room, fresh candles, and sparkly lights. You deserve to romanticize your life!

♏ **Scorpio:** Loyal, ambitious, intuitive. There's no stopping a Scorpio on the move. But we're begging you to take a breather, and fuel yourself with food for the body and soul. A fruit + chocolate combo is the perfect way to show yourself some much-needed love.

♐ **Sagittarius:** Compassionate, assertive, optimistic. You bless everyone in your life with a contagious positivity, but often fail to reserve that energy for yourself. Take a break from the screen and try an activity (like reading, writing, or knitting) that settles your mind, and requires no social interaction.

♑ **Capricorn:** Disciplined, practical, sensitive. You put your all into building yourself a beautiful life, but then completely ignore self-care. Make it make sense, Cap! Slather your body in a bougie moisturizer, give yourself a mani-pedi, just indulge in all things you deem "frivolous."

♒ **Aquarius:** Independent, easygoing, intellectual. You're an expert at spending time in isolation, but that can get suffocating sometimes. Moving your body with intention is the perfect way to refocus your energy. Ditch the high-energy cardio, and try a mindful yoga sesh, outdoor stroll, or some dynamic stretching.

♓ **Pisces:** Selfless, empathetic, engaging. You're a master of giving all you have to the people you love . . . and that's great and all, till your tank runs empty. You def need a personal decluttering session to recharge your batteries. Strip the sheets, fold the laundry. A clean room = a clear headspace.

Signs You're Ready to Date Again

Picture this: No more crying when you hear their name. None of that doomscrolling or stalking on IG. Just peace. Birds chirping. A soft violin. Bliss.

Yes, this magical vision of peace can be yours . . . for the small price of six months (to a year?) of reflective healing and personal epiphanies. No biggie. But srsly, when going through a breakup, your ex occupies 95 percent of your mental space, leaving no room for the real you. Over time, that cloud slowly fades away, until you're left with yourself again! Woo!

So how do you know you've achieved this magnificent accomplishment? Here are the five signs you're ready to start dating again:

1. You have your own life (a.k.a. hobbies, friends, dreams, ambitions)!

2. You don't immediately think of calling your ex to cope with your emotions.

3. You rationally see the positives and the negatives in your past relationship.

4. You've set new standards and intentions for future dates/lovers.

5. And most importantly . . . you feel excited about dating again!

If you're in the midst of a difficult breakup, these goals can seem quite out of reach. But you WILL get there. Start with baby steps, like picking up old hobbies and calling friends when you feel low. Day by day, the overwhelming thoughts fade away, as you rediscover the beautiful, chaotic, thrilling world of you!

When One Story Falls,

The Signs as Types of Friends

motivational friend
ARIES

loyal friend
TAURUS

busy friend
GEMINI

loving friend
CANCER

funny friend
LEO

wise friend
VIRGO

everyone's friend
LIBRA

cool friend
SCORPIO

wild friend
SAGITTARIUS

inspirational friend
CAPRICORN

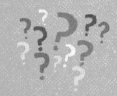

curious friend
AQUARIUS

intuitive friend
PISCES

FRIENDSHIPS

Have you ever noticed that your friends were all born around the same time? Coincidence . . . or just astrology?

Astrological compatibility isn't just for romance, kids. It's for friendships too. Like, there might very well be a reason why your Virgo gf isn't keen on your Gemini bestie. Just saying.

From Leo, queen of the squad, to Aquarius, a.k.a. Phoebe from *Friends*, every sign comes equipped with its unique friendship persona. And yeah, astrology can't *guarantee* friendship chemistry, but it can totally help you navigate behaviors, personalities, and personal preferences.

Regardless, friendships take work! You gotta nurture them if you want them to last, just like any other relationship *RIP Tamagotchi*. So read on for our grade-A tips and tricks to make the most of your cosmically ordained friendships.

Communication

LIBRA: Hey, so it kinda hurt when you flaked on our plans yesterday.

SCORPIO: I'm so sorry! I was actually just feeling really low. It really wasn't personal.

LIBRA: You can always tell me when you feel like that. I completely understand where you're coming from and I'm here for you.

SCORPIO: Thanks, girl. Lucky to have a friend like you. 🥰

LIBRA: Same. 🖤

Ahhh, yes . . . communication. The buzzword of the century. Everyone *thinks* they're an expert communicator until they realize they've repressed every tear since 2002.

When it comes to friendship, communication is truly key. And it consists of more than gossiping and giggling (although that's important too!).

Both Libra and Scorpio often fall short in the communication department 'cause they really don't like confrontation. At all. They'd rather passive-aggressively ignore your texts than actually admit to being annoyed.

And unless some serious changes are made, this friendship will quickly fade. Libra has to pack away that shallow (yet charming) conversation, and dive into the heart of things. We know this air sign has a lot goin' on up there. Now's the time to keep it real.

Meanwhile, Scorpio should access that emotional side. Their guarded heart is hesitant to let any walls down, but once they do, it's like a damn tsunami. And there's absolutely no shame in the feelings game.

When these two friends figure out the whole communication issue, they are able to see the world from a different perspective. They just gotta be conscious of their own avoidant habits and be careful about stepping on each other's toes. With a little more self-awareness, their friendship is destined to blossom.

FRIENDSHIP QUALITIES
the Signs Look for 👀

★ = MOST IMPORTANT ★ = VERY IMPORTANT ★ = IMPORTANT

We all face our own challenges when it comes to making new friendships, be it fear of rejection, or maybe you're like us earthies and you don't really leave the house? No matter your obstacles, playing to your strengths is the way to go. Read on for the deets . . .

EARTH SIGNS (Taurus, Virgo, Capricorn): For earthies, friendship is a science. The formula for attracting an ideal pal? Plain and simple: go outside. You'll meet your BFF at school or work. Ya know, somewhere practical. Just don't wait three years before actually hanging out.

FIRE SIGNS (Aries, Leo, Sagittarius): Bored with the locals? It might be time to break out your passport and do some friendship sightseeing. Your bestie will be waiting patiently, croissant in hand, beneath the Eiffel Tower. And please, don't be late.

AIR SIGNS (Gemini, Libra, Aquarius): Head on down to that giant music festival and you might just find your next victim . . . sorry, friend. Your bestie is most certainly the charming crowd surfer with the rainbow fringe. And yes, your friends can be just as cool as you are.

WATER SIGNS (Cancer, Scorpio, Pisces): Find your next forever friend at your local beach, hiking trail, or outdoor garden. You need someone you can meditate and chill with, you know? Flex your empath heart . . . it will take you far! Just try not to fall in love (again), okay?

NOT TOXIC

Pop music is just so innovative right now.

I don't think innovative is the right word. Maybe predictable?

No, it's innovative.

I studied music in school. This isn't innovative.

It hurts my feelings when you correct me. I want to be able to feel safe to express myself in our relationship.

You're right, you should be able to do that. I will be more mindful to listen to you before responding moving forward.

I appreciate you, and I will try to approach these instances more calmly next time.

Thank you. I appreciate you too.

Leo and Cap, so glad you could join us for this one. We know you're both busy with work (*Cap*) or play (*Leo*). But we just had to unpack this friendship of yours.

These two can absolutely be the best of friends. Devoted, determined, and able to learn powerful lessons from one another. But ultimately, they need to work through their differences. Because this relationship can turn real toxic if not handled with care.

Caps are super smart. Like, *Jeopardy!* smart. Ruled by logic, they're a classic know-it-all, which doesn't always bode well for our dear Leo. Leo is stubborn. So even when they're wrong, they're going to find some way or another to let you know that they're actually right. They won't back down, and neither will Cap, so it's to be expected that these two are going to clash at some point.

Capricorns may seem like robots, but they're emotional like the rest of us. They just have a lot of . . . walls. So even when they care about something, they aren't gonna always show it. Instead, they'll do it their way—with subtle compliments or acts of service. Nothing too flashy. That's going to get on Leo's nerves, big-time. Leo wants you to love them more than you love Harry Styles. And Cap, they're not about that. So Leo may start to feel like the friendship isn't worth the hype.

So here's where things get toxic. Cap could dismiss Leo's communication as drama, and Leo could react by instigating arguments to get Cap to emote. We could see these two having a painful friendship breakup if they can't get on the same page and be more flexible about communication styles.

Look, Leo and Cap, when you take a moment to thoughtfully respond to one another's point of view, you show compassion. Cap, learn from Leo's expressive, charismatic nature. And Leo, learn from Cap's thoughtful, pragmatic approach to life. The beauty of this friendship is its staying power. You are both devoted beings, committed to your relationships. And you both have the power to inspire one another to do great things. Honor your differences and you'll be friends for life.

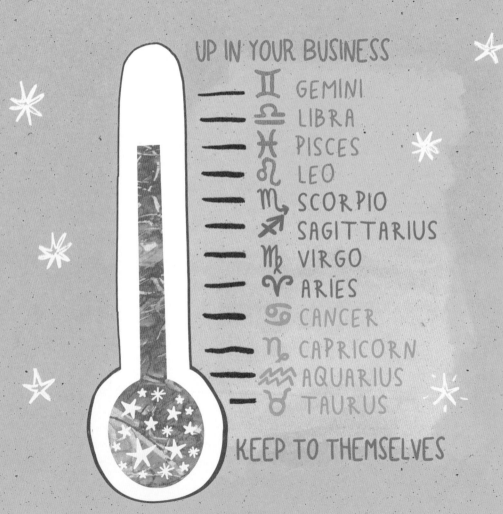

According to astrology, there are four zodiac signs that absolutely revel in a good goss sesh. Talking about others' personal lives is just good entertainment, and like, who is it *really* hurting, right? 🙄 Wrong.

Gemini should be nicknamed TMZ 'cause they always know the dirt. They promise to keep your secret, but they won't. That's why they're considered the two-faced personality of the zodiac. TBH, we're convinced they were so distracted, they forgot you gave them the "don't tell a soul" lecture. Gossip for them isn't about talking sh*t. It's for sharing what's on their mind, and sometimes, the info just sort of slips out, ya know?

Libra is a sign dedicated to relationships, and they love intently listening. But when they hear a bit of gossip, their wheels start turning. They are very concerned with fairness, but they don't always trust their own judgment. So naturally, they feel it's best to share the info with someone who can give an unbiased opinion. Yeah, they feel bad for gossiping, but it's all in the name of justice.

Enter . . . the fairest of them all, Pisces. They'll help you process whatever existential crisis you're having. But are they going to remember the story correctly? Absolutely not. These daydreamers mix and match more than Cher from *Clueless*. Their forgetfulness paired with their fear of being disliked makes them an unreliable candidate for secret-keeping. So expect a very distorted version of your story being spewed to the masses.

Of course, the notorious recipient of said gossip is Leo—because we *allll* know they just love being the center of attention. They can't help it, the spotlight just sort of finds them. Whoops? Leo is who everyone spills their guts to because they're just so darn strong, compassionate, and frankly, unaffected. And they just might keep your secret . . . for twenty-four hours.

Truth is, we all feel we need to express ourselves and sometimes, that form of expression is gossip. Don't act all high and mighty (*Capricorn*), we all do it. Unfortunately, although it may seem harmless, it's a pretty toxic habit that should be broken. Think about the consequences and if it's really worth that brief high. Because gossip is a dangerous weapon.

How to Be a Good Friend

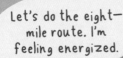

A friendship between Aries and Leo is kinda like a night out in Vegas. It's either really good, or *really really* bad. *Cue the mugshots.* But srsly, these iconic besties can get really heated . . . and that can be super amazing, or slightly scary.

As long as both fiery parties focus on being a good friend, they'll make it out okay. Both Aries and Leo are born leaders, and this can make things difficult at times. They gotta check their pride at the door and learn how to simply listen.

Their combined source of never-ending energy leads to lots of wonderful moments—and terrible, horrendous, earth-shattering disagreements. It's important that these passionate preachers avoid "sticking to their guns," and learn to truly listen. Explosive arguments create long-term resentment if not resolved with shared kindness and respect.

Despite their brave face, Leo is insecure about a lotta stuff. Aries recognizes this, and should encourage Leo to tackle the world and be the awesomest version of themselves (Is *awesomest* even a word? Let's make it one.) In return, Leo pushes easily distracted Aries to actually finish their projects.

Leo might get kinda peeved at Aries's need to be in control, and Aries might find Leo's persistence a little annoying. So here is where honesty comes into play. To avoid that sneaky pest called resentment, these friends gotta stay open with their feelings. That means no attacking their pal with random outbursts of pent-up anger. We know, easier said than done. Especially for fire signs.

Aries and Leo both need to remember that friendship doesn't require leadership. It's all about the give and take. With their synergistic energy, and mutual respect and adoration, these fiery pals are destined for friendship greatness—as long as their pride takes a back seat!

ARIES + LIBRA

GEMINI + AQUARIUS

SCORPIO + TAURUS

Best Friends

LEO + SAGITTARIUS

CANCER + PISCES

VIRGO + CAPRICORN

ARIES + LIBRA: The fearless and feisty Aries perfectly balances Libra's chill energy. A truly passionate friend, Aries pushes Libra to take chances and live life on the wild side—staying in on a Saturday is NOT an option. These two are basically destined for fun (yet safe) adventures and a lifelong friendship.

TAURUS + SCORPIO: Taurus and Scorpio may be opposite elements, but they got more in common than you'd think . . . like being absolute ride or dies. With Taurus's ambition and Scorpio's passion, there's no stopping these iconic besties. While other people might see them as a stubborn duo, these friends know that consistency is key to success.

GEMINI + AQUARIUS: These air sign besties are a match made in heaven. They share ALL the same interests, so the fun is literally endless. You'll find Gem + Aqua tripping over themselves laughing in the middle of crosswalk (do not recommend) or fighting for first putt at mini golf. Where these two lead, chaos always follows . . . and we're not mad about it.

CANCER + PISCES: These are essentially the iconic besties you see in every 2000s rom-com. Compassionate, silly, easily able to navigate one another's fairly strange and complex emotional roller coasters. Creative, vulnerable, and loyal, these two truly have an award-winning friendship. One that most of us won't understand, granted, but they will cherish forever.

LEO + SAGITTARIUS: Simply put, these two are lifelong soulmates. They'll laugh, they'll cry, they'll destroy their shared enemies . . . You know, all the healthy components of a fun and crazy friendship. Sag loves listening to Leo and Leo loves tagging along on Sag's wild and unpredictable exploits. Together, this dynamic duo will take on the world.

VIRGO + CAPRICORN: An immediate harmony is found here. These two are dedicated to the same cause—productivity and purpose. Together they'll explore nature, pursue their dreams, balance their checkbooks . . . Virgo will admire Cap's ability to get things done and Cap will appreciate Virgo's focus. It's the practical, secure relationship psychologists dream about.

FAMOUS DUOS

♓ PISCES

♌ LEO

Rihanna +
Cara Delevingne

♐ SAG

♋ CANCER

Taylor Swift +
Selena Gomez

Sofia Vergara +
Reese Witherspoon

♋ CANCER

♈ ARIES

♒AQUARIUS ♊GEMINI

Harry Styles +
Stevie Nicks

♊GEMINI ♒AQUARIUS

Courteney Cox +
Jennifer Aniston

Mindy Kaling +
B.J. Novak

♋CANCER ♌LEO

FAMILY

From your overbearing sister to that cousin who always competes with you for attention, you have an array of star sign personalities in your family. And yes, they aren't always the easiest to deal with, but that's what astrology is for! You can read up on their sign, get to know them a little better, and gain some insight into how this crazy family dynamic works. This is true for your chosen family too. Because your family is your home—that group of people you feel safe with and loved by, whomever they are. And you have a very important role in their lives. So sit back, relax, grab some eggnog, and let's dive in.

SIBLING INTERACTIONS
Love + Support

SCORPIO

Hey. Haven't heard from you in a bit. R u good?

Ya, just figuring things out with work. Stressful.

CAPRICORN

SCORPIO

Let's FT. It always helps to talk things out.

I'm free to talk tmrw. Ty

CAPRICORN

SCORPIO

Nope. Calling now.

Siblings (n): Built-in besties . . . if you play your cards right. Everyone knows that sibling relationships can be a rocky road. But they can also be the best thing that ever happened to you. Sometimes nobody can understand you better than someone who shares your DNA.

While Scorpio and Capricorn may seem like an unlikely duo, they both make the BEST siblings. Our emo Scorp is excellent at expressing emotions, and they take pride in their ability to communicate. Instead of nasty fights and accusations, they sit down with their sib and talk things out, straight up.

Slightly less emo Cap struggles to express their feelings in an open and honest way. Luckily, sista Scorp saves the day, practically yanking the emotions from Cap's guarded soul. (Don't worry, it's not as scary as it sounds.) Cap recognizes Scorpio's magical ability to unearth (no pun intended) those deep-seated feelings. And they return that love by always helping their sibling with little tasks and projects. Acts of service is Cap's field of expertise.

From childhood to adulthood, this feisty duo will have each other's back. They share a mutual respect and understanding that will tie them together, no matter where their lives take them. This is a bond to really cherish and nurture. 'Cause like all good things, it takes work to maintain. But the end result is SO worth it!

SIBLING INTERACTIONS
Arguments

VIRGO: y r u going out tonight?

AQUARIUS: wdym

VIRGO: project due tomorrow? U failed the last one . . .

AQUARIUS: ur not my mom. Leave me alone.

VIRGO: k then. Ruin ur own life

There's nothing like a sibling to (passive-aggressively) criticize all your flaws! It's like a built-in microscope analyzing every move you make. Especially when it comes to a Virgo's wrath, the heat is ON—and Aqua melts under that pressure.

Virgo just hates watching their siblings make the same mistakes again and again and again. Their rational minds can't understand this self-fulfilling cycle of doom. Listen, Virgo, sometimes your beloved siblings HAVE to fail (a lot) on their own before actually being successful. No amount of pushing or criticism will build them into the perfect person (a.k.a. another Virgo).

Emotional Aqua takes Virgo's critiques quite personally. This conflict pushes Aquarius further into a little hole, as they rely on ice cream and cozy blankets to comfort their sadness. Listen up, Aquarius. The only way to fix this issue is straight-up conflict. No, not the screaming and yelling type of BS. There's actually such a thing as productive conflict, a.k.a. confronting Virgo with a non-accusatory mindset. Use lots of "I" statements and avoid language like "you did this."

With a little bit of effort on both parts, Aquarius and Virgo can nurture a lasting sibling bond. If fighting ever escalates too far, it's important for this combative pair to take a step back to collect their thoughts. They both have very sharp tongues, and risk saying something hurtful in the heat of the moment. With the right mindset, these feisty sibs can build an enduring relationship (and team up against their parents for some epic family drama).

GETTING ALONG:

PARENT/CHILD

Aww, Taurus and Pisces. A parent-child bond that's just made for each other. Yes, these two are the perfect balance. The Taurus parent is gentle, loyal, a true protector. The Pisces child is sensitive, affectionate, and supportive.

When it comes to parenthood, "stability" is Taurus's middle name. They'll do everything they can to make their children (and the rest of the fam) feel as safe and secure as possible. Taurus is encouraging, hard-working, and of course, generous. Like, Taurus's house is probably the most beautifully decorated on the block. And don't get us started on the charcuterie-grade snacks . . . divine.

Taurus wants their home to be a source of solace, something their imaginative, sensitive Pisces child craves in order to fully express themselves. Taurus is fascinated by Pisces, the charming weirdo of the zodiac. And yes, sometimes Taurus just goes with it, playing along with Pisces's whimsical, yet not always rational way of thinking. But often, when Pisces lacks common sense ('cause they're just so darn trusting), Taurus intervenes. Because Taurus is NO pushover, able to see through everyone's BS.

Yes, Taurus has a great deal of wisdom and of course, patience, but let's be honest, Pisces has more. Taurus often gets worked up, losing their cool over mundane things like traffic, tardiness, or low-quality sushi. Luckily, our little patient Pisces is there to calm them down, for there are few who can see past the often harsh and critical demeanor of Taurus than Pisces.

Pisces is more forward thinking then their set-in-their-ways Taurus parent, who is skeptical of the *new and improved*. Yes, we get that vintage sounds fancy Taurus, but sometimes, you just gotta get with the times. Pisces sees the beauty and potential in the modern—something Taurus can learn a lot from.

Taurus wants to be someone their children look up to, especially dreamy Pisces, who inspires them daily. Pisces is excited to absorb all of Taurus's important life lessons, like the value of a dollar or how to pick the perfect produce. And yes, these two are starkly different, but that's what's so cool about their relationship—they encourage each other to explore the world out of their comfort zones. A dynamic we could all learn a lot from.

ARGUMENTS:

PARENT/CHILD

You know that extroverted mom who secretly wishes their kid preferred pom-poms over books? Yeah, that's what you call the Libra parent + Cancer kid dynamic. Nobody asked for it. Nobody likes it. But you gotta handle the cards you're dealt. And at the end of the day, it's not *that* toxic.

Libra parents are social butterflies, always connecting people and creating conversation. So when shy little Cancer popped out of the womb, Libra was shocked, to say the least. Unlike sociable Libra, Cancer's energy is drawn inward, as they prefer pondering deep thoughts and dreams.

The logical Libra parent misinterprets this introversion as selfishness . . . when it's *really* not. Libra will use every trick in the book to try to connect with Cancer—cue the torturous shopping trips where NOTHING is purchased. Over time, Libra's gotta realize that Cancer is not easy to change. And they shouldn't have to! Libra should try reaching into Cancer's universe and show interest in their personal hobbies. Cancer may initially resist this intrusion, but anything is better than being forced to try on itchy clothes.

The Libra parent admires Cancer's creative mind and dedication. Although Libra doesn't quite understand these artistic inclinations, they should express interest and provide support. But remember, there is a fine line between support and pressure! Let Cancer move at their own pace.

As Libra steps back from pressuring their kid, Cancer might feel kinda abandoned. We know, it's a catch-22. Cancer longs to feel loved, but also craves independence. To achieve this fine balance, Cancer needs to learn how to express their needs, as well as their boundaries. You have a strong voice, lil crab. Now you just gotta use it!

This sensitive and intuitive parent-child duo is prone to conflict, but it's nothing a little bit of effort can't fix! It's important for Cancer and Libra to connect on an emotional level, without any ulterior motives. Rather than forcing an awkward shopping date, Libra should try casually catching up with Cancer, showing interest in their personal activities. These little moments of connection will help build a strong and authentic relationship.

MOST LIKELY TO:
Astro Family Edition

Most likely to be the soccer mom or dad

Most likely to overdo it on back-to-school shopping

Most likely to cheat during your family Monopoly game

Most likely to be the wine aunt

Most likely to know all the family secrets

Most likely to pull a prank on you

Most likely to be a
helicopter parent

Most likely to
embarrass you in
front of your friends

Most likely to
unintentionally criticize
your appearance

Most likely to lecture you
about finances

Most likely to crash the
family reunion

Most likely to
"borrow" your clothes
without asking

IF YOU WISH TO LEARN MORE

Congratulations, you've completed Relationship Astrology 101! Everyone gets a star! If you enjoyed your experience, we invite you to continue your cosmic journey by venturing past your zodiac sign. There are so many other planets and aspects to explore. From the moon sign (which deals with emotions) to your rising sign (which influences the way others see you), astrology is filled with exciting intel into who you are.

And while we're basically astro-geniuses, we barely touched the surface, so we encourage you to dive deeper—learn more! We hope this little book of ours piqued your interest and gave you some valuable insight into how the signs act in relationships. Now, take this knowledge, and convert all your friends and family into astro-fanatics. But don't forget about us. We miss you already.

  THE JUST GIRL PROJECT

ACKNOWLEDGMENTS

Thank you to all the fans, followers, and friends of The Just Girl Project. We wouldn't be here without your unwavering support. We are consistently inspired by the amazing community you have helped us build over the years.

We would like to thank our parents, Laurie, Rick, Paula, and Steve, for always believing in us and encouraging us through every obstacle. We would not be here without you!

To our siblings, grandparents, partners, friends, and pets: thank you. You are the backbone of our ambition. We so deeply appreciate your support.

To our endlessly talented illustrator, Erica, thank you for working so hard to support Just Girl and for creating beautiful pieces of art that speak to so many young women. Your dedication and talent do not go unrecognized.

And finally, thank you to our hardworking publishing team, who were our greatest cheerleaders during this journey.

ABOUT THE AUTHORS AND ILLUSTRATOR

ILANA HARKAVY is the founder of The Just Girl Project—a girl power magazine and artistic movement that empowers readers to embrace their passions, be blatantly honest, and take ownership of their individual struggles. Along with Just Girl, Ilana runs Nailed It! Media, a SoCal creative agency. She resides in Los Angeles, California, with her dogs, Camden and Winnie, and her husband, Collin. A self-proclaimed astro-junkie since university, she runs a weekly astrology podcast with her best friend called *The Vicious Virgos*.

BRIANNA RAUCHMAN is an avid writer and illustrator who began her writing journey in third grade designing homemade books. Throughout her life, she's faced struggles with mental health, and found writing to be a critical outlet. As a freshman at UC Berkeley, she discovered The Just Girl Project and was instantly inspired by the empowering content. She immediately hopped on board as a content creator, connecting with girls across the globe. She lives in Los Angeles, California, spending her free time writing, reading, and drawing.

ERICA LEWIS is an illustrator and designer based in Dallas, Texas. She is a graduate of the Rhode Island School of Design and creates surface pattern designs, social media graphics, and editorial illustrations from her home studio. She has been illustrating for The Just Girl Project since 2019, and loves making work that people can relate to and take inspiration from on social media. She also loves the color pink, drinks too much coffee, is constantly bingeing TV shows, and lives for walks with her pomapoo, Bella.

Printed in China

SPRUCE BOOKS with colophon is a registered trademark of Penguin Random House LLC

26 25 24 23 22   9 8 7 6 5 4 3 2 1

Text: Brianna Rauchman
Illustrations: Erica Lewis
Editors: Sharyn Rosart and Jill Saginario
Designer: Alicia Terry

Library of Congress Cataloging-in Publication Data is available

ISBN: 978-1-63217-437-6

Sasquatch Books
1325 Fourth Avenue, Suite 1025
Seattle, WA 98101

SasquatchBooks.com

MIX
Paper from
responsible sources
FSC® C169962